The Shapes of Light

Also by Ian McFarlane and published by Ginninderra Press
Evening at Murunna Point
Of Cheese & Chutney
Aspects of Empathy (Pocket Poets)
A Bold Concept (Pocket Polemics)

Other books by Ian McFarlane
The Jerusalem Conspiracy
The Siberian Sparrows
Shadows

Ian McFarlane

The Shapes of Light
rediscovering poetry in a post-poetic age

The Shapes of Light: rediscovering poetry in a post-poetic age
ISBN 978 1 74027 844 7
Copyright © Ian McFarlane 2014

First published in this form 2014
Reprinted 2016

Ginninderra Press
PO Box 3461 Port Adelaide SA 5015
www.ginninderrapress.com.au

Contents

Foreword	11
Preface	13
Birdsong	23
The Apple Tree	24
Carnal Knowledge	28
Chess	29
Copenhagen Climate Caper	30
Lament for Marysville	31
Lost Horizons	32
Prompted by Acorns	33
The Philistines	34
Twenty O Three	35
Paradise Mislaid	36
Some Brief Notes on Capitalism	37
Melancholia	38
On Being Lucky	39
Asking for Trouble	40
Chance Encounter	41
Teaching the Black Dog Punctuation	42
Leaving the tent	43
The Shapes of Light	44
Doubtful Songs	45
Shadows	46
Terror Nebulous	47
On Waking at 3 a.m.	48
Echoes from Treblinka	49
The Boundary Rider	50

Crying at Funerals	51
A Lament for the Third Millennium	52
Epiphany	53
The Chosen World	55
Seen Dimly Before Dawn	56
Winter Love at Wallaga Lake	57
The Girl on the Railway Platform	58
Annie Dreaming	60
The Jazz Singer	61
Hooking the Flipper	62
Good Manners	63
The White-faced Heron	64
Thoughts from a Pantry	65
Democracy	66
Living Dangerously	67
Listening to Silence	68
The Black Snake	69
Aspirational Voters	70
The Mountain and the Eagle	71
The Cliff Path – Then and Now	72
The Post 9/11 Neo-cons	74
Evening at Murunna Point	75
Chances	76
A Country Town Koori	77
Covert Racists	79
Short thoughts from a long night	80
Midnight Cantos	82
Ink spots	83
White-collar Red-neck Greenies	84
The Children of Babylon	85
The Chardonnay Elite	87
Asylum Seekers	88
Reconciliation	89

One Small Step	90
The Outsiders	91
The Sentimental Socialist	92
Meeting Mary	93
Solitude	94
Playing Safe	95
A Theory of Dust	96
In Praise of Growing Old	97
The Last Laugh	98
Islands	99
Journal notes – 11 February 2009	100
Clown's Dice	101
The Case Against Economic Rationalism	102
Remembered Love and Other Things	103
I Spy	104
Optimal Illusions	105
The Sounding Bell	106
Some Sunday Afternoons	107
Remembering John Shaw Neilson	108
Daybreak	109
Virtuality	110
The Perfect Poem	111
Elegy for a pre-digital world	112
Whispers	113
On Losing the Plot	114
Playing the Game	115
The Picnic	116
Endgame	117
In Vino Votive	118
Remembered Trees	119
Beyond the Reef	120
The Redeemer	121
Unexplained Happiness	122

The Other God	123
Inside Running	124
Lament for a Greenhouse	125
Civilisation	126
Words that Might have Been	127
Twilight	128
Winter Waves	129
A Close Run Thing	130
First Person Imperative	131
The Case Against Knowing Too Much	132
Familiar places	133
Death of a Muse	134
Catch Twenty-two	135
Blessed is the Fruit	136
Goblins	137
Imagination	138
The Taste of Rainbows	139
Cassandra	140
Benediction	141
The Playing Fields	142
An Unsolved Crime	143
The Reverence of Apples	144
Global Warming	145
On Reading Poetry in Literary Magazines Today	146
The Sandbank	147
Gulaga Breathing	148
To Write or Not to Write	149
On being weary	150
Last lines	152
Epitaph	153
Acknowledgements	154

For the memory of my dear friend, the passionately irrepressible jazz singer, Madam Pat Thompson, whose love of poetry, social justice and politics, conversation and laughter were worth more to me than Prozac

Foreword

Having had the privilege to publish a great deal of Australian poetry, I can confidently say that, as a mode of expression (if not as preferred reading matter), poetry in Australia is in vigorous health. As they have for centuries, people are turning to writing it as a way of understanding and dealing with the moral and personal concerns and crises with which they are beset. Many use it too to celebrate the simple joy they derive from the natural world and the personal relationships in which they are involved. It may be argued that some of it is not as good as poetry used to be or as poetry ought to be, or even that it would better not be called poetry at all, but that would be to overlook the fact that the world is constantly changing; the poetry that comes out of it need not be expected to mimic, or even to emulate, the poetry of the past and it ought not to be – cannot be – judged by the same criteria. However, some of it at least is as finely crafted and as capable of stirring emotions, stimulating thought and shedding light on the human condition as anything written in the past. Moreover, simply as a phenomenon, modern poetry should be applauded as evidence of a very healthy breadth and diversity of cultural participation that arguably hasn't been seen in previous generations – exactly the thing, in fact, that Ginninderra Press has for more than sixteen years sought to foster.

For all its generally unheralded contemporary ubiquity, however, and not withstanding the evident quality of poems such as Ian McFarlane's in this volume and Ian's passionate belief in the power of the form, poetry is unlikely to succeed, as he wishes it might, in reclaiming the kind of place it had in the time of Wordsworth, Tennyson or Neilson – less for reasons to do with its quality or its preferred forms than by virtue of the fact that poetry of any kind is unwelcome in a mass-media-saturated world. The reading (and the writing) of it requires a stillness and reflection that money-driven mass media rightly fears, lest it break the consumerist trance in which those media seek to entrap us all. All the more disappointing, therefore, as Ian laments in his preface, that many modern poets choose to shroud their work in point-scoring obscurity at a time when clarity and accessibility might encourage more people to read poetry and thereby find an opportunity to escape the pernicious clutches of mass media.

When you spend a few hours with the poems in the following pages, you'll discover how easy it is, and how deeply satisfying, to escape the mass media trance and savour the wisdom, compassion and insight of a shamefully neglected voice in contemporary Australian poetry.

Stephen Matthews

Preface

It's a good idea to define your terms before attempting an opinion about anything, but since poetry is one of the most subjective of all the arts it staunchly resists objective classification. Suffice to say, the heart of poetry is more than any definition could possibly make of it, and leave the rest to take care of itself.

In fact, poetry has always been many things to many people, but an embarrassingly lopsided writer/reader equation has driven it underground, to pub and coffee shop live performance, or the cyberspace shadows of website production and blogs. Paradoxically, back on the surface, in an increasingly crowded, complex and confusing world, there appears to be little trouble filling print anthologies, finding prize money or maintaining a vibrant (if incestuous) Ozlit debate on poetry's definition and purpose.

However, an inconvenient truth remains: there are many more people writing poetry than there are reading it, and the sad irony of this Great Poetry Dilemma (GPD) concerns the way insiders probably have themselves to blame, although very few are prepared to acknowledge the possibility.

Maybe it's time we pushed back the furniture, cleared enough space to swing a few theories, and got down and dirty by cutting to the chase. We need poetry in our lives for the same reasons we need music, or the visual arts: to help gather the social and cultural sustenance to nourish a collective imagination capable of carrying us beyond the twenty-first century. But first we must somehow reach a shared understanding about what and where poetry currently is; why it is failing to engage us in the way it once did; and how we might rediscover its curiously redemptive therapy.

Most people can recognise poetry when it is attempted, but few seem able to agree - if contemporary examples are any guide – on what it becomes when it succeeds; although, measuring something as dangerously subjective and seductively affecting as poetry in terms of success or failure is to miss the point. Poetry simply is. Or it isn't. And why it is or isn't has to do with the context and aspiration of those responsible for its creation and existence; many of whom seem to have forgotten that poetry lends itself to celebrating the senses before the cerebellum.

Having tested the basis of poetry's allegedly intrinsic difficulty over many years, and grown increasingly impatient with glib variations of the cop-out response – 'If you want to communicate use a telephone' or the disingenuous diversions of so-called 'language' poetry – I'm sufficiently pissed-off to suggest that poetry today is unread because much of it is unreadable. And I'm referring here to more than just a suspiciously arrogant dismissal of meaning – a poet can be forgiven for sometimes hiding in dark corners – it's also the deliberately awkward structures and discordant rhythms that casually jar the eye as well as the ear.

We're drilling near a GPD nerve, so it might be sensible to apply the anaesthesia of some common ground before the pain kicks in. Obviously, good poetry is more concerned with asking questions than finding answers, and inclined to cast a jaundiced eye on the deep and dark stuff that stalks us all. Any aperture focused to this degree of acuity will naturally block light strong enough to supply two-plus-two-equals-four illumination. However, this doesn't mean the reading room should resemble a coal cellar at midnight during a power cut. The remains of a candle can usually be found, tucked away at the back of a cupboard, if you're prepared to look – sadly, most contemporary poets aren't.

Using metaphor and allusion to turn the screws on language to summon up a sense of that beyond the reach of dictionary definition has poetic validity; pushing a barrow load of arcane bric-a-brac cloaked in wilfully suffocating obscurity doesn't. It merely locks the castle gates with a self-conscious suggestion of teasingly, catch-me-if-you-can cleverness, and seldom rewards the effort of close reading. Frankly, I've always been appalled by the notion of poetry (or any art, for that matter) as a puzzle to be solved, rather than an enriching experience to be enjoyed, and applaud Sam Johnston's robust response: 'Difficult, Sir? I wish it were impossible!' Obscurity makes demands on the reader; clarity makes demands on the writer. Obviously, there's an important distinction to be drawn between clarity and simplicity, but I passionately believe it is possible to be a 'serious' poet and still be understood. It's just a damn sight harder.

Poetry offers a conversation with the imagination of anyone prepared to listen, although this presupposes a level of accessibility acceptable to both sides of the partnership.

Of course, one of the chief problems with trying to pin poetry down has to do with its abundantly various forms: from the bush ballad's bouncing banality to the measured discipline of a sonnet; the gnomic economy of haiku; and the tediously ongoing rivalry between free verse and lyric rhyme. Robert Frost once memorably compared writing free verse to playing tennis without a net, and – as a tennis-playing sometime poet – I'm inclined to agree, although I'd have to also confess to dabbling in free verse. Let's face it, who hasn't?

Until quite recently, rhyme was crime and sniffingly discarded from the poetry editor's slush pile, preferably with a pair of surgical tongs. Now, I'm beginning to suspect the postmodernists are hedging their bets by adding a nip of shy rhyme to their sly crime; driven home, as it were, by the eye-opening splash of a toe being dipped into the icy water of comprehension. Heady stuff, since serious poetry (in other words, that likely to be found in little lit mags) was hitherto inclined to fear clarity as politicians fear honesty; which evokes Oscar Wilde's quip about intelligibility finding you out.

I grew up in a beautifully rural backwater of 1950s post-World War II England, close to where Tennyson lived and wrote much of his poetry. Not surprisingly, as a child falling rapidly in love with the sounds and patterns of words, I feasted on his lines like a hungry seagull: 'Only reapers, reaping early / In among the bearded barley, / Hear a song that echoes cheerly / From the river winding clearly, / Down to tower'd Camelot' and many more of similarly mesmerising ilk. I'm certainly not saying all poetry should sound like this – poetry does what it can, in whatever form best suits its mood – I'm merely pointing out that, for most people, this represents ground zero. And we do well to remember that lyric rhyme is easy to do badly, but very hard to do well.

Poetry is the mother tongue of language, but requires the kindness of a good teacher to nourish its voice. My primary English teacher wasn't kind; she was a memorably joyless woman of indeterminate age, who one day asked each of my class to choose a poem we enjoyed reading. A week later we were summoned, one by one, to stand alongside her, at the front of the class, to recite our selections. Most were predictable, having been harvested from the school library children's anthology, but I chose a poem from a battered volume of collected verse found on my father's makeshift shelves. It was Tennyson's heart-wrenching expression of grief – 'Break, break, break, / On thy cold grey stones, O Sea; / And I would that my tongue could utter / The thoughts that arise in me' – but before my faltering tongue could utter much more than the first stanza, I was brought to an abrupt halt by the teacher's imperious command: 'Wait!'

In the awful silence that followed, she turned towards me, her previously weary and long-suffering expression awakening into a frown. 'Why did you choose that poem?' she asked.

I stared at her in terrified confusion. Because you wanted me to, I might have replied, but could find no words.

'You chose it,' she said, her eyes unblinking, and lips drawn back to reveal an improbable abundance of teeth, 'a few moments ago, at random, because you had forgotten to do as I asked last week. Is that not so?'

I shook my head, managing a barely audible whisper: 'No, Miss.'

She stood up, reaching, with sharp-boned fingers, for one of my ears, and twisting it painfully. 'Then perhaps you'd be good enough to tell the class precisely why you chose it.'

The silence stretched towards infinity, as hot and stifling tears of humiliation stung my eyes. What did I know of metrical beat, strong and steady as a healthy young heart? What did I know of the siren song of cadence? I wasn't even aware of the word. I had chosen that poem because I liked the moody sound of its almost hypnotic rhythm. A simple enough explanation, if only I'd been able to give it a voice. But I just stood there, struck dumb by fear in front of my classmates, wishing I was somewhere else. And very soon, I was: bundled into the exile of a draughty corridor and made to stand alone, reflecting on my unexplained sin, until the morning milk break.

A lifetime later, I'm slumped at my desk, on the far south coast of NSW, pecking disconsolately at a brief review of a novel about poetry — *The Anthologist* by Nicholson Baker – and enjoying momentary distraction from darker thoughts with the playfully satiric notion that rhyme provides poetry's true form. I'm also buoyed by Nicholson Baker's whimsical definition of poetry as a 'controlled refinement of sobbing', and the way his plausible correlation between music and poetry reminds me of John Shaw Neilson, a sadly neglected Australian 'rhymer' whose life and work deserves to be remembered.

John Shaw Neilson was born in Penola, South Australia, on 22 February 1872 and died in Melbourne on 12 May 1942. He received little formal education and most of his life was occupied by hard physical labour. The first of seven children, he was soon burdened by the weight of caring for siblings and never married. Nicknamed Jock by family and friends, he called himself Shaw Neilson to avoid being confused with his father, also named John and a sometime poet. Jock was an itinerant labourer, wandering the flatlands of western Victoria and often distracted by having to help his family survive a dreary succession of crop failures, bad debts and tragedy, as they toiled in search of a dream of rural independence that was never fulfilled.

John Shaw Neilson's poetry has a curiously other world quality that resists definition. It was shaped by the 'thunder blue' God of his mother's stern Presbyterianism, his father's tireless good grace in the face of overwhelming hardship, and a

Celtic love for the sound of words as well as their meaning. The pastoral transparency of his verse has been too easily pushed into the background by the bush-hardened masculinity of Henry Lawson and Banjo Paterson.

Neilson's classroom was the natural world and his instinct was to seek the lyric dimension of its expression. When first discovering him many years ago, I couldn't understand why he was so neglected. I still can't. And it hurts to hear people recite Lawson, Paterson and Kendall without knowing a line of Neilson. His talent was intuitive and compassionate, untainted by formal education and flowing from an anonymous and relentlessly impoverished life. He was always going to be hard to explain.

Some years ago, when the ABC ran an audience survey seeking a favourite love poem, I suppose it was inevitable that a few lines given celebrity status by a popular movie would come out on top. But I wonder how many of the people who voted for Auden's 'Stop all the clocks', having heard it in *Four Weddings and a Funeral*, would have been aware of an Australian love poem containing these lines: 'Her eyes foretold of happiness / As grapes foretell of wine: /Her feet were as the lights that fall / In greeneries divine.'

I suspect literary criticism falters in the face of Neilson's unexpectedly profound poetic imperative. There's a sense of shock, almost of offence, as if he had somehow been successful in a task for which he wasn't qualified. His verses are a spider's web of words, diligently spun in some more innocent and gleaming dawn, all fragility and light. But strong enough to do the job. A stanza from his poem 'Song Be Delicate' could well be his credo: 'Let your song be delicate / The flowers can hear: / Too well they know the tremble, / Of the hollow year.'

All of which suggests, in ways similar to Mozart's music being beneficially compatible with elemental human tempo, that we are naturally predisposed towards rhythm and rhyme. And, like it or not, reawakening a few traditional elements is more likely to lure poetry back to mainstream literary status than discordantly cryptic broken lines. The postmodernists don't have to close up shop, just ease off for a while, giving something more accessible a chance to seduce us into the forgotten pleasures of quoting lines aloud, or at least remembering them for longer than a few moments.

The further poetry reaches into its potential audience, the closer it comes to recording 'the still, sad music of humanity' in ways likely to enrich and strengthen our sense of community.

We are prisoners of our perception. We see what we expect to see, and often get it crucially wrong. My distantly remembered English teacher lacked the imagination to see beyond her conviction that I had failed (or even worse, ignored) her assignment because she refused to accept that a nervous eleven-year-old boy could have chosen a poem of such adult sophistication for any reason other than a last-minute stab in the dark to avoid being exposed as lazy or forgetful. The truth was far less contrived, but much more profound: I had chosen that poem because, at a particular time and place, it resonated, emotionally and linguistically, with an intricate web of things, seen dimly before an adolescent dawn and conjured into being by the less than two per cent of our genetic make-up that separates us from the chimpanzee. The cerebral cortex has validated humanity by granting us the extraordinary gift of abstract thought, reflected from fireside stories told in caves, to the fearful wonders of industrial, cultural, political and technological revolutions, and the healing redemptions of love and forgiveness. And all the while, poetry – as a brazenly original and humanising use of language – was part of the amazing journey.

Choosing that long-ago classroom poem has faint but indelible links to the choices we must now make with our planet slouching towards hell in the hand basket of global warming; pre-emptive war; environmental vandalism; corporate corruption; financial meltdown; and religious, political and racial intolerance. A consummate, chaotic and potentially catastrophic mess caused by the triumph of greed over imagination, and compounded by the emotional and intellectual sterility of a terminally banal popular culture.

We need, more than anything else at the moment, a flint to spark some creatively lateral solutions. Poetry can't save the world, but rediscovering its humanity can maybe help us find something that will.

Ian McFarlane
Wallaga Lake, NSW

The spring is wound up tight. It will recoil of
itself. That is what is so convenient in tragedy.
The least little turn of the wrist will do the job.
Anything will set it going: a glance at a girl
who happens to be lifting her arms to her hair
as you go by; a feeling when you wake up on
a fine morning that you'd like a little respect
paid to you today, as if it were as easy to
order as a second cup of coffee; one question
too many, idly thrown out over a friendly
drink - and the tragedy is on.

Chorus, *Antigone*, Jean Anouilh

It is the bright day that brings forth the adder…
  Brutus, *Julius Caesar* (Act 11, scene 1), William Shakespeare

Birdsong

For the children of Newtown, Connecticut, who were murdered by a stupid law

Our cloth is cut against the grain,
to resist sweet reason's will,
by legalising weapons
designed primarily to kill.

And a child in the school yard
staring down the sun
is stolen by a nightmare
configured by a gun.

While a blackbird in the pear tree,
as evening sidles in,
sings as if our tired old world
were entirely free of sin.

For we pin the stars at sunset
to empty days long flown;
and miss the chimes at midnight
coming closer to the bone.

The Apple Tree

'There comes a moment in each childhood when a door opens and lets the future in.' – Graham Greene

In that other country of the past,
there is a farm;
abandoned as a result of unrecorded tragedy,
and rambling into weed-haunted wasteland,
where wild creatures roam,
and claim sanctuary to raise their young.
It's a far and lonely place,
on the edge of an old forest,
where few people have any cause to visit.
Behind the farm, and pressing hard
against the trees,
as if trying to escape some large
but nameless cruelty,
is a long-neglected orchard full of apples,
betrayed by market forces and forgotten.
Apples with elegant and graceful sounding names:
Egremont Russets, D'Arcy Spice, Lord Lambourne,
and the Beauty of Bath.
They're lost and gone forever now,
like street kids shooting drugs,
their gangling growth unpruned,
and fruit rotting where it falls.
In the middle of the orchard
stands the highest tree, thick-stemmed
and twisted with age.
But still bearing the sweetest fruit:
glowing in the dusk
like tiny crucibles of fire.

In scattered dreams, which may
or may not reflect reality,
I scramble through a broken fence
after school and munch on apples
like some contented beast
ignorant of its guilt.
Then I climb the highest tree,
right to the very top,
and rest in a cradle of sheltering leaves.
From where I can see the farmhouse roof…
and a curl of smoke from one of its chimneys.
The place has been empty for years,
and my flesh tightens under a knife-edge
of sudden fear,
causing the tree to shiver around me,
as if disturbed by beating wings.
But I'm well hidden, I tell myself;
is it possible anyone can know
that I am here?
Below me, the tops of smaller trees
stretch away like the surface
of a rippling field of wheat.
Empty and silent.
Except for the soft thud of a wary footstep,
that drags my gaze downwards like a startled bird.
But it's just a falling clutch of over-ripe apples,
coming to rest among dappled grasses
as winter moons on frozen and forgotten seas.

I look up again, and to the east,
the forest darkens
into silhouette and shadow.
And to the west, beyond the farmhouse roof,
with its unexplained ribbon of grey smoke,
a big, yellow sun is masked by vaporous cloud.
Giving off the tawny sheen of sweet water
running down through honey.
I catch my breath,
sensing the closeness of unknowable things.
Feeling them move around me,
like the folds of a dark and voluptuous cloak.
Whose touch is gentle;
yet as strong as a discovered poem,
or a picture,
or a piece of music,
that makes you feel as tall as Christ,
even though you don't know why.
I gaze beyond the farmhouse roof,
towards the horizon, like an eagle watching for its mate,
and a sudden coldness falls upon me,
as the future dreams me into life.
I can feel it breathing – all around me in the air,
as if coming from the apple tree itself.
And I am re-born at the age of twelve,
seven metres high above the ground,
cradled by a tree that nobody wants,
and watched by an empty farmhouse with its chimney
of culpable smoke.

I climb back down,
to a world that looks unchanged
but will never be the same again.
And neither will I.

Carnal Knowledge

The quickened breath
and willing tongue
recalled the weight
of church bells rung;
in meadows
haunted by the sound
of sacrilege
on Holy ground.
And chastened
by so bright a fire
he sought to sanctify
desire –
as the surface tension
of this pause
betrayed the hunger
of his cause:
from the acquiescence
of her eyes
to the Neptune cradle
of her thighs.

Chess

Play reflects personality, and although
inclined to cloister my bishops,
I've always enjoyed a certain frisson
of extravagance with my knights.
The patterned elegance of a mid-game
board, with its serial threat
of fatal combination,
has the still and dangerous beauty
of a Greek tragedy – if, for example,
knight takes bishop and rook
takes knight, will my queen,
suddenly released from her
cordoned sanctuary, and sweeping
imperiously over rank
and file, seriously threaten
mate in three? My hand pauses,
as the knight waits
for its God to move.

Copenhagen Climate Caper

Final Day – October 2009

Dawn invokes dissension
With a brooding sense of shame
As climate change dimension
Fans a global flame.

Morning sessions waver
On deconstructed themes
Clinging to the favour
Of disingenuous dreams.

High noon strikes the table
With the tolling of a bell
Extinguishing the fable
That everything is well.

Nightfall signs the paper
With a hand that barely shakes
Pleased to close the caper
Before the Kraken wakes.

Lament for Marysville

February 2009

Eucalypt and mountain ash,
etched against a blood-red sky,
crushed beneath the summer's lash,
and withered by a futile cry.

This daydream town of dappled light,
cloaked by forest, deep and green,
lies wasted by an awful blight;
empty, brooding and obscene.

The seductive curve of shopfront path,
the tea and scones of rustic charm,
are embers in the aftermath
of loss and deeply rooted harm.

Can autumn days cool the pain?
Shall passing years temper grief?
Regrowth buds will shoot again,
and the ash will green the leaf.

Lost Horizons

A suburban sonnet

Morning beckons, curtains sway,
shadow shapes begin to play
our footsteps to the waiting train,
grumbling gently yet again.
Through weary suburbs weeping light
from window eyes of secret fright,
to day long rituals in a scheme
of crunching numbers on a theme,
we gild a landscape from our time
with mountains we will never climb.
And in the evening, homeward bound,
like penitents on holy ground,
perhaps we glimpse the seldom found –
our lost horizons, all around.

Prompted by Acorns

It's a lifetime since I climbed the oak tree
in order to escape myself – almost with regret –
as if leaving behind an embarrassing friend.
In wasteful dreams, where branches claw at clouds,
and castellated leaves dance the vortex
of impatient youth, the mystery is secure;
seen dimly, before dawn, like a Jackson Pollock canvas,
bent on salvaging one last glorious song
from the sackcloth of its passion.

So, I climb again – like Sisyphus with the boulder –
steeped in the corruption of a deconstructed world.
For what we leave behind defines us with a keener eye
than what we take away. But now, at the other end
of things, I find the tree is smaller,
but the risks greater, and meaning much more tenuous.
Perhaps redemption is a turning leaf,
thirsting for its sacrament of water –
and what remains is little more than compost.

The Philistines

They watch commercial TV,
listen to radio shock jocks,
seldom read books,
and vote for stupid laws.
Their credo is the urban myth, with its siren song
of fatuous but plausible half-truth.
They believe themselves to be decent,
hard-working and honest (and often are)
it's what makes them so invincible.
But they're afraid of the dark,
and fearful of what they cannot understand.
And what they fear they learn to hate.
And what they hate they try to destroy.
They'd be a joke if not for the fact
that their collective voice usually
decides who runs the country.
They're impervious to reason or example;
try telling them they're wrong; that the way
they do things is not how civilisation works,
and they'll tell you to piss off; accuse you
of being a Chardonnay socialist, a bleeding heart,
or part of some intellectual elite
that wouldn't know its arse from its elbow.
These people are untouchable. They rule the world.

Twenty O Three

(A retrospective on Iraq)

T r u t h
was murdered
by a lie
that shook the earth
and burnt the sky

On TV screens
we watched it die
AND DID FUCK ALL
to question
why

Paradise Mislaid

Do you recall that summer
we found the empty beach,
trapped between a headland
and the forest's closing reach?
And how you said we'd beachcomb
to escape the awful world,
and live on love and oysters
to keep our flag unfurled?
And how we threw our mobile phones
so deep into the sea,
and drank the stars at midnight
with the joy of being free?
So long ago, so far away –
so innocent – so yesterday.

Some Brief Notes on Capitalism

Frankly, I find it bizarre that freebooting capitalists
are frequently also God-fearing Christians,
since – apart from anything else –
I have little doubt (based on what I've heard)
that Christ today would be at least a socialist,
and possibly (God forbid!) a communist.
Capitalism has three fatal flaws that hardly
anyone bothers to notice, let alone consider:
firstly, it presumes that everyone wants to take part,
and penalises those who don't (or can't);
secondly, it claims that everyone can succeed,
which is nonsense, of course, since the system
wouldn't work if all of us made vast amounts
of money. Capitalism requires a fall guy,
and every bean counter knows that the best way
to make sure the rich stay rich
is to make sure the poor stay poor.
And thirdly, the essential function of capitalism –
making money from money – is ethically vacuous,
since it nourishes greed, celebrates self-interest
and fosters aggression, division and war in a world
desperately in need of cooperation and community.

Melancholia

He wasn't where they found him,
with their flickering lamp of hope;
deep inside his realm of twilight,
on the cradle of a rope.

They cut him down with silent wonder,
since he was burnt without a mark;
running wildly, but not moving,
like a shadow in the dark.

They took him to that point of distance,
trapped between the yin and yang
of fanciful illusion,
and back before it all began.

They tried to find the place he came from,
but that, of course, could never be;
so they found him something closer;
between making do – and misery.

First published in January 2010 in Volume 28 Nos 1 & 2 of the
Australasian Journal of Psychotherapy

On Being Lucky

Further along the dinner table
the talk is of hospitals and operations.
Of how one of us has been placed
under the surgeon's knife.
The woman at my elbow
inclines herself in my direction,
as if sharing something valuable,
and whispers, 'doesn't that make you
realise how lucky you are?'
I turn away, knowing she is waiting
for my nod of affirmation;
for words that might release the empty weight of
consolation. 'You're right,' she wants to hear me say,
'I am lucky. Clinical depression is nothing compared
to having your chest sliced open by a razor.'

The evening ends and car doors slam,
as invisible guests carol their goodbyes.
I pause on the way out;
feeling the sting of midnight
make the first of a thousand cuts.
Each one unseen,
and sharper than the last.

Asking for Trouble

For where is here?
And when is now?
And how are things to be?
For why is this?
And who is that?
And what will set me free?

For this is how things really are
How thinking makes them so
When the sky has lost its colour
And there's nowhere else to go.

For I have seen eternity
And borne its midnight brand
On endless days repeated
In a single grain of sand
I have crossed its lonely desert
And sailed its frozen sea
I have lingered where the winter dark
Has cast its eye on me.

And all I ever wanted
Was honey still for tea
Honey still for tea.

Chance Encounter

He seems familiar, like someone
I should recognise: thinning hair,
unruly in the dry heat of a summer breeze,
and shoulders slumped, as if disappointed by life.
Or wearied, perhaps, by the burden of carrying
too many years that don't care to be remembered.
He lowers his eyes to avoid mine,
and sudden fear, like a beating of caged wings,
crowds my vision.
All this, in the few seconds it takes to realise
that he is a reflection of myself;
trapped by sunlight bouncing from a shop window,
and already turning away, embarrassed and confused.
I glance back over my shoulder in time to catch him
doing the same thing, although he looks more anxious
to avoid my reality than I am to escape his.

Teaching the Black Dog Punctuation

Heavier than weight
pulled by the flood tide
of a razor-edged moon,
I curve with the caution –
of a comma,

Trapped inside the dissonant pain
of a fingernail scratching
across a blackboard,
I stall with the lethargy –
of a semicolon;

Crushed on the anvil of reality
by the unforgiving oblivion
of wasted words,
I am silenced by the brutality –
of a full stop.

But lifted by the honeycomb wing
of a distraction large enough
to escape the sting of death,
I take flight with the joyous escape –
of an exclamation mark!

Leaving the tent

Do you know where I went?
When it all became so unhinged,
the lights went out, and I had –
for want of a more biologically
accurate description –
'a breakdown?'

Oh, I know where I went, physically;
I even have an idea of where I went,
psychologically. But where did I go –
existentially?

Metaphorically, I'd left the tent,
saying, 'I may be gone for some time,'
but in reality I hadn't moved
(which was probably a mistake)
and inclined to believe
that nothing had happened
(which was definitely a mistake.)

Because everything had happened –
all at once.

The Shapes of Light

Trapped in this labyrinth of despair,
and haunted by its shadows there,
light flutters, restless, on the wing;
dark, unleashed, and beckoning.
A sadness bows the watcher's head,
the Black Dog wakes and leaves its bed.
The die is cast and gathered on;
the half-light settles, like a swan.
Then sometimes sweetly on the tongue,
like first love tasted by the young,
the shadows move and fall away;
as redemption lingers with the day.
The light becomes a shawl of lace,
full of beauty, depth and grace,
and once where only demons stood,
there is a pathway through the wood.
But out beyond the shapes of light,
caught in that labyrinth of the night,
the Black Dog guards its secrets well;
cast in bronze and burnt in hell.

We don't see things as they are,
We see them lit by our own bright star.

Doubtful Songs

I know that you know
that they knew about it,
and that she said that he said
that they said 'don't doubt it.'
But frankly, I wonder
what has ceased to be true;
between telling him, telling her,
and finally you.

For we seek to remake
as we travel along;
remembering the singer –
not always the song.

Shadows

For the memory of climate change rationality – 2012/13

Come fetch me in the evening,
when the fools and tyrants leave,
and we'll talk of that forgotten
from what remains to grieve.

Perhaps we were merely phantoms
to those beyond our reach,
and although they paused before they ran,
there was nothing left to teach.

And now a silence beckons
from the undiscovered night,
as truth becomes the sacrifice
of reason's failing light.

Our footprints fade and vanish;
the endgame has begun,
and lost inside a wilderness,
we face the searching sun.

Terror Nebulous

For the first Australians

Caught on the unforgiving cusp
of a conqueror's perception,
in light from a star that no longer exists,
they become visible only in the accretion
of small things. For which there are no words.

They blink at the millennium;
with its dysfunctional shapes
of reconciliation and regret.
And quietly drown in the shadows
of a reconstructed history.

Waiting for their indigenous Godot.

Listening for the ticking
of his ancient blood.
In a story so endlessly untold,
even Beckett would have baulked
at the prospect.

On Waking at 3 a.m.

A dream skitters towards oblivion,
leaving a scurrying sound
outside the bedroom window;
chasing its own echo
into the half-resentful silence
of an autumn night. One of those
fragile and very still nights,
where the smallest sound is magnified.
Was it a possum? Probably;
I don't believe in ghosts, and have few
possessions likely to attract thieves.
I raise my head and listen –
to the steady rhythm of sleep-filled
breath from the pillow
next to mine, and beyond that
a rolling sigh of waves on Camel Rock Beach.
Something moves. It's the clock radio,
flickering to three-zero-zero,
and my head slowly returns
to the pillow. My eyes close, and I wait –
for sleep, dawn or death.

Whichever comes first.

Echoes from Treblinka

For the victims of terror and oppression

The SS guard who stood at the gas chamber
door and ripped open the bellies
of pregnant women with his bayonet
wasn't the devil. He was one of us.
With a mother who probably loved him.
His actions were evil because he was sadistic
not satanic. And conceived by a system
of institutionalised arrogance that nourished cruelty
in order to appease its own corruption.

He still exists.
Because we lack the collective imagination
to cut his umbilical cord
by believing in ourselves,
rather than the malignant
mystery of our fables.

The Boundary Rider

In lonely watches of the night,
he passes by in smothered light.
Gleaming with all passion spent,
In promises unkept but meant.

And distant echoes of repent.

The muffled door and creaking stair,
are torn from nightmares cradled there.
This is how our great world ends:
With dreams and sins and absent friends.

And desperate hopes to make amends.

Crying at Funerals

(For Marjorie)

Sometimes the grief is loaded,
sometimes the tears are slight.
Sometimes a troubled conscience
casts a weary light.

But when the moment trembles
on its rim of boundless chance,
a lifetime trapped in amber
is released within a glance.

I touched my mother's frozen face;
it was smooth and waxen dry,
but when her world was fastened down,
I'd forgotten how to cry.

A Lament for the Third Millennium

For Indigenous Australians

Their days came down with darkness,
and nights that saw no moon.
Their language lived before mine did;
their dreamtime woke too soon.

For they were claimed without a cause,
and formed without a face;
their songlines in another voice,
their lands another place.

And lacking these they loiter
with misconstrued intent,
like ghosts forsworn to wander,
or vagrants paying rent.

And they will not be reconciled
by lies or lack of will;
their story will be told again,
resonant and still.

Epiphany

First light dusts the bedroom wall,
and somewhere in the garden a bird lifts me
with the careful vigour of its song:
clear and fluted, like a rising passion,
that cracks against the air and dies.
A whip-bird, his jaunty crest
dancing the tangled hedges
by the possum-scarred gum tree.
Where the brash and busy wattle birds
chase with darting wings.

I take my cup of black, unsweetened tea,
to a sheltering deck behind the house;
grey boards dappled by the willow,
and trailing honeysuckle haunted
by a sudden memory of flowers.
The air is cool. And cathedral-still.
No human sound desecrates its silence.

A bright wedge of Wallaga Lake glimmers
between the branches of a plum tree
and the white magnolia. Pelicans drift
upon the tide like ghostly and forgotten sails,
as if towards a sea that you and I once knew.
And loved with all the careless hope of yesterday.

I rest upon the wicker sofa with its broken
strands, and cushions which you stitched
so long ago, and try to remember where
it all began: this fractured and malignant light;
this aspect of a ruined life.
This desolated time. Its stolen sleep
falling my eyes like scales.
In the prison cell of a tyrant,
where the unshaded bulb of consciousness
can never be switched off.
And birdsong is unknown.

The Chosen World

We choose to live in a trivialised world, for which
we must all share the blame. Our perception is framed
by thirty-second news grabs and smart-arsed headlines,
in a system that distorts reality into nibble-sized chunks,
selected with prejudice, and firmly glad-wrapped against
the bacterium of truth. Information becomes kaleidoscopic,
accuracy hit or miss, and motivation geared to the cash register.
We're provided with cosy little glimpses of everything;
from tax cheats to test-tube babies; sporting triumph to
cataclysmic disaster; corporate greed to the obscenity
of starving children; street corner punch-ups to pre-emptive wars,
and substance abuse to suicide bombs. We glance and look away,
assuming we know what's going on. We don't. We haven't even
scratched the surface. We're breeding a new generation
of philistine: shallow-minded, materialistic and self-interested.
No wonder bigotry and intolerance take such
healthy root. No wonder racism is institutionalised.
No wonder religious fundamentalism threatens to cast us back
to the Crusades. No wonder Western imperial arrogance
is breeding hatred faster than a speeding virus. No wonder the
rain forests fatally diminish, and we continue to poison our
environment. No wonder global warming looks likely
to finish us off once and for all. No bloody wonder.

Seen Dimly Before Dawn

The dust-grey shards of splintered light,
the yesterdays of hope;
the prison bars of shackled night,
the scraps of hangman's rope.

The dead cold ash of wasted scheme,
the turning burning fear;
the shooting star of childish dream,
the quick and restless year.

When springtime danced its promise strong,
and summer coursed with heat;
when autumn keened its dying song,
and winter dragged its feet.

Now light is lost in shapeless thought
between night and fruitless day;
and judges in their secret court
have nothing left to say.

Winter Love at Wallaga Lake

For Mary

We drink the wine and eat the bread,
and not a careless word is said.
The water laps like fabric spun
from forests full of silent sun.
Listening for the quickened sigh,
the trees draw down and crowd nearby.
The lake is flecked with grains of gold,
the light is squeezed through air grown cold.
The dreaming mountain moves above,
and steals the sunlight from our love:
flesh ensleeved in one black coat
on a bed of sheoak cast afloat.
Tangled warm with rhythmic pace,
we free the silence of the place,
as beating wings fade soft away,
and hushed, we linger with the day.
The lake is bronze and silver cast,
the trees are phantoms of the past.
We leave like thieves treading light
through the shadows of the night.
The ancient shore, now safe alone,
returns its dreamtime to the stone.

The Girl on the Railway Platform

Alone with the sting of constant stress,
and already defeated
by a short and brutal life,
she struggles to control two young children.
Her face, once pretty, is pinched and defensive.
Her eyes, once friendly and wide,
are narrow and sly. She moves with the wariness
of a caged animal; trapped by a system
that says she is responsible
for things she doesn't understand.

Although herself little more than a child,
she's a mother now, and her innocence
(which she doesn't care to think about)
is long gone; a starship flight away.
But it's not just disenchantment,
no, it's something worse than that,
far worse, something almost sinister.
As I watch, she catches my eye
with what seems like a brief
and silent plea for help.
But instantly it's gone, and suspicion sets in.
You're part of it, I see her thinking,
you, and your well-dressed wife.
Going into town with money in your pockets.
She looks away, and I know she's found it necessary

to cheat the system in order to survive.
In her world, honesty is a sign of weakness.
In her world, relationships are traded
for the best possible return,
like any other commodity.
In her world, there is no music,
no art, no books, no poetry to embalm the pain.
She's alone and trapped and doesn't know why.
It's all there; the process is etched
into her skin like a concentration camp symbol.
It's shot through her body
and comes to the surface
in the downward slant of her mouth,
the slump of her shoulders,
and the raw, defeated look in her eyes.
She's been betrayed by life,
and banished to an underworld
without compassion,
where nobody cares what happens to her.
And she doesn't know who to blame.
That's the nub of it really;
there is no one…
except, perhaps, all of us.

Annie Dreaming

For a schoolgirl who dived, laughing, into shallow water

Somewhere in the scheme of things
there is a song that darkness sings,
to soothe the ghosts beside her bed
who whisper memories in her head.
Pleasures, innocent of earthly sin,
cast shadows of what might have been,
as shapes of beauty lost and deep,
nibble at the edge of sleep.
When morning comes she wakes and finds,
regretful day behind the blinds.
As seasons change and kinships call,
and when her face turns to the wall;
there'll be no song that's worth redeeming,
half as sweet as Annie dreaming.

The Jazz Singer

For the memory of Madam Pat Thompson

She haunted talk-back radio after midnight;
chasing red-neck fear and prejudice
into darkness. She deconstructed
postmodern poetry, economic theory
and right-wing Christian fundamentalism
with playfully passionate wit.
Her crusade for social justice
spanned prime ministers, presidents
and governors-general, and she belted
out the blues with an exuberant love of life.
She could make you want to stay around;
and her irrepressible laughter
meant more to me than Prozac –
because she was my friend.

Hooking the Flipper

A very postmodern poem*

'Bollocks!' cried the vicar, helping himself
to a virtual scone while Mrs MacTavish
powdered her Facebook and took middle stump.
Snowflakes could be heard falling
as Shane Warne delivered a cleverly flighted flipper,
which Mrs MacTavish hooked sweetly
over square leg fence with obvious satisfaction,
before adjusting her iPad and regarding
the vicar with surprise. 'Are you still here?'
she tweeted through knitted teeth.
'Apparently,' he replied, dunking his smart phone
into another can of strawberry worms.
'By the way,' he added, licking the screen with
a forked tongue, 'that ball wasn't short enough to hook.'

*A form favoured by inner circle literati, who might be inclined to consider the above example as follows:

Discuss ways in which iconic images of popular culture have been used to penetrate the existential nihilism of deconstructed socio-economic paradigms by exposing the quasi-political variables of a deracinated class system in a post-industrial and multicultural society.

Good Manners

It's almost certainly unwise
to fudge the truth and generalise;
or take a one-dimensional view
that separates the me from you.
And it's probably not a good idea
to over-think that grain of fear;
far better sense in wider scheme,
to push beyond the selfish dream,
and seek a torch to cast a light
to guide us through the rushing night.
Because drifting down without a name
floats an echo from a wider game,
that deep within its hidden core
beats chaos on our fatal shore.

The White-faced Heron

Pale and sleek with eerie grace
he passes by in slender face.
And as he moves he seems to share,
a depth of silence lingering there;
suggesting we are all involved
with this great labyrinth yet unsolved.
What unseen vision does he bring?
Whose pages do his stories sing?
And does he sense the higher sky,
that cloaks my elevated eye?
In which context do we meet?
What confluence guides our passing feet?
He knows I watch him, I can see
the secret ways he watches me.

Thoughts from a Pantry

Reaching for a tin of sardines, I notice
the jar of treacle, unopened, and well past
its use-by date. Purchased in a burst
of nostalgia for parkin – an esoteric
ginger cake my mother used to make,
on the other side of the world,
long ago and far away. In fact,
when Baghdad was still a storybook town –
where a princess might live – and America
a brash young salesman with one foot
in every door. And I forget my sardines on toast,
with freshly ground pepper
and finely chopped parsley, and remember
only the splintering hatred of a suicide bomb.

Democracy

From city hall to outback shed
With pencil stubs of hopeful lead
The punters make their sanguine mark
Like gypsies dancing in the dark
And as the ballot boxes swell
With paper scraps designed to tell
The wanted from the least preferred
The harmless from the most absurd
A tattered freedom is unfurled
In a godless and corrupted world
And politicians far and wide
Including those we know have lied
Nod and smile and turn away
Happy their dog has had his day.

Living Dangerously

For the compassionate wisdom of Laurel Lloyd-Jones

To beat back intolerance,
in a time and place
that is – and equally – is not
amenable, is to risk suspension
between what we know of form,
and what we believe of substance;
like a leaf caught on the cusp
of a dangerous definition.
Because hubris defines compassion
in a way that disenchants hope –
however, to understand the leaf
with what we know of love,
is to seek all we need to know
of wisdom.

Listening to Silence

I sometimes worry
If I might
Disintegrate
Within the night

And drifting slow
Inside this dream
Listening to
Its silent scream

I wonder why
I'm here not there
Now not then
Or anywhere.

The Black Snake

By the potting shed a grassy path
leans against the light.
And drinking in the golden sun:
the shivery scales of night.
Long and sleek with sinuous will
he lays uncoiled and very still.

Watching me as I watch him;
frozen with the day.
Wondering at the scheme of things
and who has right of way.

Then he moves with liquid speed:
an urgent, thrilling grace.
Vanishing as the sunlight fills
the flickering hollow space.

I stand alone upon the path
his image cold and clear.
Which will I remember first,
the beauty or the fear?

Aspirational Voters

They talk reverently of financial advisors;
can rattle off interest rates
and property prices as if speaking in tongues,
and are likely to dismiss the left
as a sanctuary for failure.
After a few drinks they might
tell jokes that demonise welfare cheats
and lionise tax cheats. But they cherish
their children, don't usually kick dogs,
and remember their mothers.
The trouble is, their world of
'sound economic management'
is too narrow for things that are difficult;
such as poverty, prejudice and pre-emptive wars,
or the social conscience of a half-way decent
democracy. For them, everything is reduced
to a balance sheet, where survival
becomes a commodity,
and compassion a fluffy embarrassment,
like crying at sentimental films,
or feeling sorry for the handicapped.
These people represent the new Jerusalem:
they are proudly independent…
and fatally indifferent.

The Mountain and the Eagle

In liquid light on wooded slopes,
Gulaga is weeping:
A Henry Moore sculpture
of a woman sleeping.
An eagle on the updraft
from Wallaga's sandy mouth,
mocks the law of gravity
with breezes from the south.
Waves curl towards the entrance
in question marks of foam;
the mountain and the eagle
are redefining home.
Flags of myth and moment,
and culture gathered wide,
shape a new republic's anxious hopes
from symbols of her pride.
But Gulaga's ancient valleys
whisper secrets of their own;
beyond the pale of history
and chilling to the bone.
The eagle falls with blurring speed;
dark blood rips the prey,
and dreaming in the sunlight,
bright shadows rim the bay.

The Cliff Path – Then and Now

But at my back I always hear
Time's winged chariot hurrying near.
– Andrew Marvell

Captured by a searching sea,
the child runs,
as if carried by the wind,
headlong down a low, rambling cliff,
through trees haunted
by the rasp
of pebbles feeding on the tide.
Leaping the sun-baked rifts
of winter's sinuous clay,
stumbling, breathless and giddy,
and rushing on,
swept up by the sense
of being two people;
one travelling faster than the other.
Head and shoulders
pulling the slower feet
of someone else.
Someone lost within the perfect joy
of running so fast,
he cannot catch himself.

*

Now, a senior citizen of sorts,
but disinclined for its diversions,
he moves to strike a tennis ball,
while coming to the net,
or walk the afternoon away
into the evening edges
of a different sea.
The long land brooding
with its short history
of a closer past.
And sometimes with the light upon the cusp,
that fleeting moment when the world is true,
he sees the child,
ahead of him on the path,
running at the distance
like a shadow from the sun.
And glancing backwards
into his future;
as if afraid
of being caught.

The Post 9/11 Neo-cons

They believe in the Bible,
sometimes literally so,
and take comfort
from the righteous anger
of occasionally smiting their foe.
They regard themselves
as a force for good
in an evil world,
quickly becoming impatient
with opinion other than
the cast-iron hubris
of their own cause.
They see doubt as a weakness,
and hold the greatest sin
to be government interference;
regarding the marketplace
as able to set its own paradigm.
They'd be cardboard crusaders
if not for the shock and awe
of their global power.
These people arguably constitute
the greatest obstacle to the possibility
of human redemption
since the first stone
was cast in anger.

Evening at Murunna Point

The grassy twilight deepens
on the hill above the bay,
the sea is dark and washed by cloud
in the haunting of the day.

Gulaga broods against the sky;
a tapestry of light,
her green and darkling shadows
beckoning the night.

On the lake a blue crane wades
with sad and secret grace,
treading the sandbars of a dream
inside some distant place.

A moment caught by beauty drawn
from byways strange and still,
no vanity disturbs this peace
on the path across the hill.

Chances

Is there any reason,
other than the metaphysics
of unbelievable chance
why the sky is an eggshell blue?
Is our unique intelligence
merely confirmation bias,
allowing us to see
such things as beautiful?

Did human consciousness
beat the odds, by inventing itself,
or was it really the eureka cry
of a distantly implausible God?

On a balance of probabilities,
life will survive the twenty-first century,
although we, as its historians, may not.
Unless the dice are rolled again.

A Country Town Koori

There was little in the way he stood,
or in the way he spoke,
to suggest that life was any good,
or its story not a joke.

But he slowly raised his downcast head,
and glanced me in the eye,
'I know what's happening here,' he said,
'but I don't question why.'

'You're the one who wants to know
how long the stars will shine.
Why the sun comes up and rivers flow,
and where God draws the line.'

'You think that this will set you free,
and cast aside your fate,
by granting immortality,
and closing history's gate.'

'But there's a truth you still deny,
a crime you won't concede;
and now you profit from the lie
to justify your greed.

'I have no battle to be fought,
no selfish race to win,
the only truth that sells me short
is the colour of my skin.'

And then he turned and walked away:
a sad and darkened ghost.
I saw him later in the day,
being handcuffed to a post.

Covert Racists

They'll play down the evidence as an aberration
of manners, and if challenged will respond
with aggrieved surprise, 'I'm not racist, but…'
(there's always a 'but' – actual or implied)
followed by a smorgasbord of qualifying clauses,
ranging from the pathetic to the convoluted.
These people could be anyone's favourite
aunty or uncle; a pillar of the community;
sporting celebrity, or web spinner;
they're credible because they remind us
of someone we trust; with a voice
that once upon a different time
may have sounded reasonable –
but they miss the point: racism is an iceberg,
with most of the dangerous stuff
hidden from sight; its poison seeping upwards and
outwards, like the butterfly wing of chaos theory,
until institutionalised into the violence of hatred.
They'd be appalled at the idea,
but these people nourish
the worst kind of racism: the covert kind,
that slips under the radar
of community conscience –
to diminish us all.

Short thoughts from a long night

To ask the hard question is easy,
To know the hard answer is not;
To rail against life is a given,
To find something there is the plot.

*

I sometimes think that I am bound
To chase the fox but catch the hound.

*

Life is random and unfair
There's much to haunt us from our youth
For in the evening of despair
We're told the lie but must learn the truth.

*

We seek to replace the unreachable face
Of that which can never be known
For we think we're all spun
From a collective of one
When really we're vastly alone.

*

We stare towards infinity
To see our world reflected
In the thousand fragments of a glass
Beyond the resurrected.

*

It's time to see what we can see
And do what we can do
To release the anger to be free
And find the me in you.

Midnight Cantos

I

The slow decay of nature's way
The passing into earth
The winter gain of windswept rain
The springtime of rebirth.

II

The sensuous dreams of evening
Their branches on the sky
How close they come to happiness
How easily they die.

III

The years have slipped the bridle
The bolt for freedom clean
And now there's hardly any trace
To show where they have been.

IV

A flooding tide has cast aside
The days where once we met
And futility has found a sea
To echo our regret.

Ink spots

Swept away in a corner,
where few of us bother to pause,
rests a pattern of plausible icons;
waiting for probable cause.

They have danced with the joy of a morning;
and spun on a leaf-turning breeze;
in winters of darkening solace,
and summers of wine-sparkled seas.

They thrive in compassionate anger,
but wither to drumbeats of greed;
they measure the flame from the candle,
and sift out the want from the need.

They have soared in cathedrals with glory,
or been scrawled on dark walls with despair;
but when it's all done, they're just ink spots,
and mean much the same anywhere.

White-collar Red-neck Greenies

They'll defend the popular underdog
with one-dimensional passion
born of black and white certainty,
and climb onto the back
of contentious issues of social justice
from the easiest point of access;
like flood water running down hill,
or a bushfire feeding on its own updraft.
They'll support superficial argument
with the kind of arcane,
and probably irrelevant, detail,
that usually finds enough weight to gain
a foothold on the face of mountains
they will never climb.
They posture a defence of freedom
that casts the shadow of truth on ideas
that are sometimes difficult to dispute,
but their attention span is short,
and easily deflected or disengaged,
despite often changing the direction
of social trends with perception rather than reality.
These people help form the bedrock
of any democracy: solid and sentimental –
but ultimately cracked.

The Children of Babylon

In pain and leafy jungle blood
a soldier slowly dies.
In a desert, mouth agape,
a child swallows flies.
On a small screen, sleek and warm,
a politician lies.
This is us, you and me,
deny it if you can.
We are the conspirators:
the family hood of man.

We fabricate and castigate,
rattling superstitious bones.
We justify and qualify
and speak in reverent tones.
We ease the sting of conscience
with pennies for the poor.
But in the still of midnight
we lock and bolt the door.

We glorify possessions
and see failure as a sin.
We lust for wealth and power
and blindly seek to win.
We mass produce emotions
and sterilise our tears.
We rush to careless judgement
and ritualise our fears.

We sanctify existence
with archaic Bible law.
We rationalise our hatred
and feed it into war.
We vandalise our forests
for cheap and tawdry gain.
We re-invent our history
so we can bear the pain.

Our terror of the darkness
blinds us to the light.
We see what we expect to see
and seldom get it right.

This lack of resolution
throws up a tunnel view;
that turns back in upon itself,
and kills both me and you.

The Chardonnay Elite

They invariably sniff their wine
before drinking it, although some
are not sure why. They sip latte coffee
at pavement tables, reading the
weekend book pages, and talking
dismissively of politics and ideas.
They're inclined to the left, but hardly
blue collar, with opinions unlikely
to resonate far beyond their set.
They believe themselves to be decent
and democratic (and often are) it's what makes
them holier than thou.
They delight in getting up the noses
of right-wing politicians by demonstrating
the intellectual wasteland of the neo-conservatives,
or grazing on the smoked salmon self-indulgence
of an art soirée, or the boozy book launch.
Their desire for a more civilised world is real,
but the way to hell – as GBS once warned –
is paved with good intentions.
These people assign colour and movement
to a search for substance. They can be less
than the sum of their parts, but some of their parts
can be more than themselves.

Asylum Seekers

With apologies to William Blake

To see a world in detention sand
And heaven in an excised flower
To hold a visa in your hand
And eternity in a Tampa hour.

To see children in a desert cage
Mothers wounded lacking care
Might put heaven in a rage
It leaves little mark elsewhere.

For they are forced to travel light
Chasing land beyond the sun
Trapped within their endless flight
And distant cries of Babylon.

In this new world they stand alone
Tormented by its unjust law
Downtrodden by the bloodless stone
And swept beneath its fatal shore.

Reconciliation

An awful clarity of sand
lends darkening sky a healing eye
to shape a wounded land.
Footprints bold from stories told
stretch back in captive line;
across the bay in proud display,
and culpable design.
And those who show nostalgic glow
for worlds beyond the sea;
must wait and weep before they sleep –
for ghosts to set them free.
Time is fleet, a chaff of wheat;
and we turn away – or seize the day –
with palms beneath our feet.

One Small Step

Despair can occur for reasons other
than brain chemicals becoming dysfunctional,
or life comprising a litany of frustrations
and disappointments; not necessarily connected
to an affliction that mostly goes unnoticed.
Clinical depression can occur for reasons
other than realising that God – who supposedly
made us in his image – was actually made
by us in ours, or that politicians are inevitably
weakened by power. In essence, clinical depression
can occur simply by knowing how one small step
could make the world a lastingly better place…
providing we all stepped in roughly the same direction –
at roughly the same time.

The Outsiders

They'll wallow in sentimental clichés,
about loyalty and flags,
but know little of history,
and even less of humanity.
They'll scream 'rot in hell, you evil bastard,'
as the paddy wagon removes a child molester,
but will mistreat their own children
as a rite of ancient passage,
by boozing a welfare cheque;
trashing a rented shack, or screwing
each other, factually and figuratively.
They'll use the copulative verb, to fuck,
as a noun, but demand 'clean' language
when dealing with national icons,
like Vegemite, Phar Lap or Kylie Minogue.
They've been marginalised by a system
that doesn't wait for stragglers,
and perpetuates division in order
to maintain its sense of civil proprietary.
These people have fallen off the radar,
but make a virtue of their own deprivation,
by wearing it as a badge of honour,
to taunt a world that simply…
doesn't want to know.

The Sentimental Socialist

My left-leaning stance has always been emotional
rather than intellectual, since my head
follows pacifism, but my heart the revolution.
But I'm damned if I'll be patronised
by some right-wing bastard
who thinks everything begins and ends
with economic theory, and money
always constitutes the bottom line.
Tolerance, compassion and human decency
are abstractions; they can't be number crunched
onto balance sheets, or loaded into weapon carriers,
but they belong to us all, whether we live
in a penthouse apartment, a broken-down shack –
or a cave in Afghanistan.

We are all of the same species; we inhabit the same planet;
we breathe the same air (which we have all helped to pollute);
many of us worship a similar deity (although we're inclined
to find different reasons for its manifestation).
The only faith I have now is in the healing power
of imagination and humanity,
and will extend my hand to any person, of whatever
colour, creed or culture, who is prepared to accept it in the spirit
of something greater than ourselves... Hello

Meeting Mary

The year was green and wonder seen
in every place to dwell.
But life ran deep with the unquiet sleep
of love's untasted well.

The day we met time lingered yet
in a glow of childhood truth,
and on her breast did gently rest
the innocence of youth.

Her eyes burned bright with wondrous light,
her step a vibrant thing,
and her hair spun dark with the shining mark
of a raven's midnight wing.

The world spins by, the seasons die,
and winter holds the line,
but that first day, so far away,
still tastes of summer wine.

Solitude

A love sonnet

On a day that's brushed with shining gold,
beyond the reach of winter cold,
but yet to feed on summer heat,
or relentless dust beneath our feet,
we'll find a glade beside the lake,
whose solitude we'll gently take,
and I will bring the sunlight down,
so you can wear it like a crown.
And lost inside this dream we shall
explore the fable it will tell:
from the nostalgic whimsy of its charm
to the healing comfort of its balm.
Granting us a larger truth
in which to rest our hurried youth.

Playing Safe

Poetry today suggests a game of *Scrabble*
in bad light during an earthquake,
but the literati lap it up,
like cats at the cream, or journos at a budget press release.
The two great certainties of postmodernism
are adoration of the obscure, and contempt for coherence.
Some poets fear clarity as a politician fears honesty.
To be understood is to be found out;
revealed for what you've really said,
rather than playing safe by gathering kudos
from what you're thought to have said.
Shallowness runs deep
when weighted with allusion.
Metaphors morph into metaphysics,
and symbols lend gravitas to air.
A synergy paradigm (which means
whatever you want it to mean)
usually brings home the poetic bacon;
particularly when the self-serving jargon
of literary criticism provides an alibi.

It's easy to sound clever
when no one – least of all, yourself –
knows what the fuck you're on about.

A Theory of Dust

Left undisturbed, dust will not
rise beyond a certain point.
Just as time exists
as measured by itself;
until rearranged by us
in order to know
how far we are from death.
Whereupon, time and dust gather once more
along the ledges of our lives.
Like footprints in the desert:
going nowhere –
with a sense of purpose.

In Praise of Growing Old

The modest days of gentle spring
brush the hem of summer's wing
to release a stone convention
in time to gather moss,
with words too light to mention
the weight of autumn's loss.
The candle flame is slowing,
the eye has grown less keen,
but sap is softly flowing
in leaves that once were green.
For we have told a story
that needs no winter proof,
as the rhythm of its glory
beats like rain upon the roof.

The Last Laugh

For the coalition of the willing

Here upon the night watch,
with dreams to slake the pain,
reason stops to lick its wound,
as fable flairs again.

Moonbeams run, comets fall,
shadows ebb and flow,
and softly through the silence,
there is laughter, sweet and low.

What random jest does this imply?
Taunting chaos with a song.
Who dares to claim the moment?
To whom does this belong?

A half-remembered presence –
a tired and constant proof –
of the way it always happens:
we're told lies, but learn the truth.

Islands

For the *Tampa* refugees

No man is an island,
said the poet long ago.
And yet, four hundred years later,
trapped beneath the prejudice
and fear of rejection,
spins an ocean drift
of loneliness invented
by an island so unreachable
it falls from sight every day.
As if drowning under the weight
of its own indifference.

A search for survivors was raised last night,
but could find no trace.

Journal notes – 11 February 2009

Yesterday, my GP found nothing wrong,
but today I'm tired – bone tired;
right down to the marrow
of my bootstraps:
to the intellectual and emotional
core of everything; the physical
and existential beginning and end
of my withering existence.
I'm spent, bewildered
and terminally depressed;
paralysed by disappointment
and impatient with procrastination;
suffocated by the sweet-smelling
cloth of still-born ideas
running backwards
through wet cement
towards a distant echo
of forgotten possibilities –
'I could have been a contender' –
but have finished up instead –
or so it seems – behind every
eight ball in the god-damn universe.
Apart from which – as my GP tells me –
I'm fine.

Clown's Dice

Lingering at the break of day
In dreams that chase the night away
Half asleep and half awake
With lines to write and fears to shake
Suspended somewhere in between
Where I am and where I've been
I sense a truth I want to know
Before the frantic final throw –
Life's the only game in town.
A game of dice. Rolled by a clown.

The Case Against Economic Rationalism

The quality of mercy is not strained,
said Shakespeare, long ago.
Oh yes, it is, said Marx, and others,
a few hundred years later, appalled
by the sanctimonious bastards who were sending
children down the mines, and starving
the working class into submission,
in order to make themselves
obscenely rich, and protect
a sense of God-given superiority.

Money corrupts before power,
because money is needed to achieve power.
And the palpably unfair way
society constitutes the acquisition,
retention and distribution of money,
breeds a dog-in-the-manger world
of deception and despair.

Which – in turn –
becomes a crime against humanity.

Remembered Love and Other Things

Fresh-cut grass on evening lawns;
raked with the promise
of a chilled beer waiting in the wings.
The soft, round pop
of a cork drawn before dinner
on the Cabernet Merlot,
followed by the turning pages
of a bedtime book.
And your hair – once a vibrant black, but now
a peaceful, smoke-mist grey – cast like a shadow
on the pillow.
Ice-cold orange juice, seized
with a summer sweetness,
straight from the midnight fridge.

Sharing a simple breakfast of tea and
marmalade toast; repeated, without tedium,
over fifty years of occasionally rough-stitched
but well-mellowed time. Like wearing a frayed
but favourite jacket on a winter's day.
Releasing the secret warmth
of remembered love. And other things.

I Spy

Kipling called it the Great Game;
but that was in days of Empire, when battles
were likely to have preferred starting times,
and a chance to inspect the pitch
before play commenced.
The days when a disgraced officer and gentleman
could be given a revolver and whisky decanter
(both containing one shot) and relied upon
to protect the honour of the regiment.
Times change. Honour corrupts into expediency.
Ends justify means. Undeclared war becomes
a global default setting, where shadows chase each other
in a hall of mirrors. Battles are fought
on the quicksands of paranoia.
The Great Game struggles to see without being seen.
To hear without being heard.
To break the law without being caught.
But whose law? And caught by whom?
The Great Game floats to the surface
of democracy. Weightless. And unreachable.
Like a secret that doesn't exist.

Optimal Illusions

Defeated by the silent jeers
of hypochondriacal fears,
life seems a brief and wasted space,
without compassion, love or grace.
But on the cusp of twilight calm,
with a glass of wine and Mozart's balm,
it looks so different you could swear
that demons never once were there.

The Sounding Bell

Maybe there is laughter
to spice the random tears,
but rarely is there joyfulness
in the sum of all our fears.

We conspire to use the shadows
in search of fading light,
and orchestrate our falling scales
to boost a selfish sight.

Because the emptiness of heaven,
in the crowded rush of hell,
has missed the leading question
about John Donne's persistent bell.

One day we shall stumble,
as we blindly seek to fly;
but one day we may simply live
and – just as simply – die.

Some Sunday Afternoons

Can seem as if you've just been exiled
without leaving home; like waiting for Godot
in a midnight cellar. No cricket, football
or tennis on TV; the ABC Arts program
is puffing a masterpiece that might have been
painted by an orang-utan on speed;
a slim book of impenetrable poetry,
or a concerto for three stoned crows
on a barbed wire fence. The whisky bottle is empty;
your wife is doing the ironing, and definitely
NOT thinking what you're thinking,
and you've just remembered
that tomorrow is Monday –
when the whole damn charade begins again.

Remembering John Shaw Neilson

Your restless roving days are gone;
vanished where their music shone.
Can verses of such joyous rhyme
outstrip the wounded reach of time?
For what we say and what we do,
are often used to misconstrue,
and trim the wings of those who flew.
So let us now remember you.
Your orange tree in pristine sight;
aloft within its trembling flight.
Your song, so delicate in bloom,
was woven from a silken loom.
We need your truth and tempered light
to beat against our rushing night.

Daybreak

Stretched on a midnight canvas
the dark night of the soul,
accelerates the consciousness
and demands a heavy toll.

Why can't I just release the weight,
and let the damn thing go?
Why does the restless effort
of thinking make it so?

How can the prejudiced be sound asleep?
And savages at play?
When wide awake and blameless,
I'm unjustly locked away?

An answer rises with the dawn:
despair is also sin,
and with day break all around me,
the Valium kicks back in.

Virtuality

I can still recall a time
when googling was a game;
we talked (and sometimes even walked)
to surf a different claim.
The postman carried letters
handwritten in blue ink,
and there was time to redefine,
and occasionally to think.
Now we're scrolling here,
and browsing there – and tweeting
damn near every where.
The time has come to find a pause –
and redeem the effect
by use of the cause.

The Perfect Poem

Is a blank page, uncorrupted by words,
and sanctified by silence.
The sort of stuff God would write –
if he existed, and inclined to bother
with poets and poetry today.
Which, of course, he doesn't and wouldn't;
partly because poetry has become
more about vanity than art,
but mostly because perfection is infinite –
and words are not.

Elegy for a pre-digital world

The river dies in shining mud,
weakened
by its woodchip blood.
And haunted by this forest blight,
a cottage tilts
in exiled flight.
Wind sloughs off the mountain,
breathing down a prayer for rain;
whispering words of things forgotten
to the sightless windows that remain.
The world moves on and memories vanish;
the time of wonder leaves no trace,
but by a forest-cradled river,
the cottage mourns a loss of grace.

Whispers

For politicians everywhere

If I told you
and you told me
enough to set
each other free;
do you suppose
we'd ever know
why peace declines
and conflicts grow?

Or see the differences
between
the way things are
and how they seem?

We must learn the truth
but are told the lie –
and refuse to grasp
the reasons why.

On Losing the Plot

There are so many different ways of going crazy
in a world where poverty is used as a political weapon,
and thousands of children die from starvation
every day, that I hesitate to mention the one
about trying to understand
how vacuous celebrities and corporate CEOs
can justify receiving huge amounts of money
for doing whatever it is they do each year.

If they had discovered a cure for cancer;
persuaded the Palestinians and Jews
to stop killing each other;
become actively involved with carbon reduction,
or spoken out against the treatment of refugees,
their vast reward might have meant something,
but taken in the context of global reality,
makes as much moral sense as invading Iraq,
or the claim that suicide bombers have no other choice.

*And goes some way to explaining why the world
remains such a fucked-up place.*

Playing the Game

When the key is softly turned my love
and all the songs are sung.
When all the lines are learned my love
and all the bells are rung.

When the race is all but run my love
and all the passion spent.
When the light is all but done my love
and all the veils are rent.

When all the parts are played my love
and all the stories told.
When the piper has been paid my love,
and the sheep are in the fold.

Then you and I will fall my love,
hand in hand into the flame,
knowing it was all my love
just one great and silly game.

The Picnic

We no longer bother with pre-arranged social things:
reciprocal displays of best napkins and cutlery;
the aspiring merry-go-round of well-mannered suburbia.
I suspect my wife never really understood the ritual –
which is partly why I love her – and I never really saw the point.
Now, we prefer to share a cup of tea,
and perhaps a ginger nut biscuit with family or friends;
or a glass of wine and cheese, leading – perhaps – to a meal;
prepared with spontaneity rather than fretful plans.
But best of all, is the picnic, with its sprawling chaos
of blankets and cushions; cricket bat and ball;
clinking wine glasses (the real things, of course,
despite risk of breakage) and an extravagant hamper,
that must – on pain of severe reprobation – include at least three types of cheese, a plenitude
of fresh, crusty bread, some olives…
and lashings of tolerant laughter.

Endgame

Contemporary obits draw closer
To gather me into their zone
Where existence is coyly configured
By that which can never be known.

Please spare me the words of believers
For we've rarely seen things eye to eye
Faith is no match for sweet reason
Whatever the span of the sky.

All I ask now is distraction
From such a calamitous Ark
To take down the flame from the candle
And find a way home in the dark.

One day soon when the world is not looking
And the evening is quietly complete
We'll draw back the bolt from the shutters
And sort out the chaff from the wheat.

In Vino Votive

We nose the Shiraz like connoisseurs,
although we've probably forgotten why.
The daily crossword is more difficult,
and I have to remind you that it was
Oscar Wilde not Noel Coward
who reckoned nothing made him weep
faster than bad wallpaper.
However, we take grateful solace
at being liberated from the noise
of so many irritating things,
that we smile; knowing life to be
less than the sum of its parts,
but rejoicing in the chance that
some of ours might be more.

Remembered Trees

My springtime trees of doubtful youth
were hungry for a longer view,
searching for the lasting truth,
beyond a winter's residue.
I can hear them yearning still,
like a flute song far and thin,
and taste their hunger's eerie thrill,
as a sadness on my skin.
I've travelled far and sometimes well;
I've painted dreams upon the moon;
I've sent to know for whom the bell,
and paid the piper for his tune.
But down the staircase of a sorrow,
to its core of lost lament,
creeps the shadow of tomorrow
from a passion poorly spent.
And what remains are sundry scraps,
along the fallow of a line,
with the bugler playing taps –
and the trees no longer mine.

Beyond the Reef

Evening rests upon the lake;
as gentle as a lover's hand.
Releasing a sweetly, half-remembered,
sense of home, like the blessing
from a long-forgotten priest.
I thought I could hide among
the green and restless branches
of my days forever. But I was wrong.
Now, there are distant echoes
in unexpected places that trick me
into thinking such sanctuary still exists.
But of course it doesn't. Except in memory:
that dangerous storybook of the mind,
seen dimly; beyond the reef of language.

The Redeemer

You come from a land of lost belief
And hesitate when winning
Your children live on bread and grief
And cast you out by sinning.

Across the sea and all the lands
Your shadow seeks a form
In forests and in all the sands
Your spirit rides the storm.

For you have seen the darkest place
And heard the keenest cry
Your terror has a human face
Your sorrow longs to die.

One bloody day when you are gone
And all that's left is shame
We'll find the place compassion shone
And resurrect its claim.

Unexplained Happiness

The palette of an evening cloud
explores the sky, as if floating
on the updraft of its own invention.
To glance away will let the story vanish;
like a memory of something
that is yet to happen. So I watch and wait.
Rejoicing in the manner of a thirsty land
that drinks a steady fall of rain. Eagerly.
But not too fast. Letting the colour
seep into the marrow of my senses
to express a sadness larger than the world;
like an awareness of mortality
without meaning.

But something else lingers softly
against my eyes, like a good red wine
on the tongue – an elemental quality
that has no name, possibly because
it doesn't need one, but probably
because it is the sum of all names:
the reluctant, and almost holy,
taste of unexplained happiness.

The Other God

What are we? Other than a mass
of cells within cells, given shape by flesh
upon bone. A heart that pumps warm blood,
just like any other animal,
until it becomes too tired,
worn-out or diseased to carry on.
A brain that functions in ways
we don't yet fully understand,
but choose to call human, rather than animal,
because this grants us the possibility
of a larger story.

But the human brain is a paradox
that betrays itself through reason. And dares
to suggest we are merely chemistry made conscious
by a cosmic catalyst of such incredible power
to create a planet capable of sustaining us.
And a God called Ego.

Inside Running

The web of life is spun by strife,
with an urge to jump the gun:
I don't wish to know is the chorus;
It will always be so is the song,
yet pride has slipped in before us,
despite everything else going wrong.
In the beginning it seemed like a doddle;
a breeze – an expression of fun,
then we all started to waddle,
as if our race had already been run.
Can we pass through the eye of a camel,
with light fading fast on the path?
Look! – the warden just tipped us a wink –
which shows what he'll do for a laugh.

Lament for a Greenhouse

The wasted scheme of futile dream;
the promises unkept.
The plundered seam of lofty theme;
the well of tears unwept.

The sighing sand of dying land;
the solace of the flame.
The strand by disillusioned strand;
the weary waiting game.

The carrion seed of wanton greed;
the grasp beyond our reach.
The destructive deed of righteous creed;
the hypocrisy of breach.

For this what we're really worth,
how things have come to be;
in the twilight of our planet earth -
in damned eternity.

Civilisation

Arrogance distorts so many things, it's a wonder
we even bother to notice, let alone try to understand,
the truth. We like to think we've come a long way,
from the wheel to the microchip, but we've merely
managed to somehow nudge ourselves towards the light;
like shadows on a sunless day,
and have so far left to go,
to contemplate the distance still remaining
is to invite a terrible despair.

'We are good, they are evil,' said the leader
of the Western world, with an assumption
of civilised, modern-day, morality,
that waited, like the Ancient Mariner's albatross,
for its chance to spit in the eye of truth,
with images of US soldiers behaving like medieval morons.

This is the way the world ends; not with a bang or a whimper,
but with the empty arrogance of a lie.

Big enough to betray us all.

Words that Might have Been

'A sentence uttered makes a world appear.' – Auden

Hope beyond redeeming
weaves the spent refrain
of a tired old warrior dreaming
to the beat of distant pain.
His weary voice remembers,
with disappointed tone,
the sadly dying embers
of wasted life alone.

The reckless road he followed,
the deconstructed hate;
the hubris to be swallowed
for a reinvented state.

In corridors of power,
where laws are planned and made,
his memory haunts the hour,
with the honing of a blade.

And havoc cries the headline,
as carnage fills the screen,
and doomsday tempts a deadline –
with words that might have been.

Twilight

There's a cusp upon this evening,
as light begins to fail,
that sings of milk and honey,
poured from the Holy Grail.
And in a moment time expands,
as the Black Dog slinks away;
and bitterness unravels,
to redeem the shapeless day.
But this is no epiphany;
there is no mystery here;
the twilight theme is quarried
from a single grain of fear.

Because that's the hidden secret;
the shape of second sight:
to cut adrift the darkness
with a searching blade of light –
by listening to the moment
of when and why and where,
and how the silence settles
on the cleansed and rushing air.

Winter Waves

Watchful, as the forgotten eyes,
of women drowned by lovers' lies,
an elliptic beauty carves their pride
on the rising buttress of a tide.
A solace cloaks this lonely bay,
like shadows on a sunless day;
as if in search of that between
the known world and the yet unseen.
Dimpled grey and towering white,
in whispering walls of winter light,
they break upon a futile shore,
with chaos and confronting roar.
Whose echoes beat along the sand –
of a jealously remembered land.

A Close Run Thing

The candle flickers, and fails.
Not through any lack of will
to keep it burning,
but through
a paucity of timing and tone:
a myth concealed too late,
the truth revealed too soon,
a shadow cast too softly,
or the beam of light too hard.
And the centre dissolves,
like the tolling
of an unheard bell;
deafened by the hunger
of its silence.

First Person Imperative

What might you do
if I became you?
Where would you be
if you became me?
Why should you care
whose pain we might share?
How far could we run
when travelling as one?
Assuming we knew
one travels faster
than two.
But when all is done,
can two become one?
Or are we just peas in a pod?
Each in search of a God.

The Case Against Knowing Too Much

Curtains lick my face
as the bedroom drinks a breeze,
and an owl in the tree outside the window
hoots softly once, as if
sharing a secret with a trusted friend.
The sleeping darkness waits, and
the clock radio glows two-fifty-nine.

Napoleon discovered courage in its rarest form:
at three o'clock in the morning;
the eye of the night,
when life seems least defensible, and
the veil of the temple most likely to rend
itself from top to bottom.

So I watch the flickering figures become
three-zero-zero, and
stare down a sudden fear behind my eyes,
that presses like a body of cold water
against the wall of an overflowing dam;
and shivers,
as if aware of what will happen if it breaks.

I do nothing upon myself, said the poet long ago,
but am mine own executioner.

Familiar places

I've looked behind the mirror,
where shadows never fall,
and clothed myself in moonlight
as it settled on the wall.

I've listened to the creaking fear
of loose hinges at the door;
pulsing on a night watch breeze,
between three and half past four.

I've waited for the owl to hoot,
from the tree outside my room;
and wondered if he ever knew
how sweetly flowed his gloom.

I've turned the pages of a book,
with sightless eyed repression,
and known the pain – inside the pain –
of clinical depression.

Death of a Muse

Bring down the lamp from the window,
and roll back the blind from the sill,
for morning is chasing the shadows,
and stealing the light from the hill.

Where heroes once gathered to honour
the true and the just and the strong;
the green peak lays withered and barren,
with only the wind for a song.

But echoes drift up from the valley;
dim and distant, like whispered regret,
as deep in the eye of the labyrinth,
a tyrant begins to forget.

For this is the way of the world now,
in darkness, betrayed by a lie,
where the death of a muse is forgiveness,
and redemption merely a sigh.

Catch Twenty-two

The soft, sweet sadness of ordinary life, with its borderless pain of a water torture dripping towards banality, suggests introspection.
'Forget thyself into marble,' said Milton long ago.
Good advice. Indeed. But how does one
forget oneself in a world where ego
has become so utterly essential
to the validation of human
creativity? It's a problem
of curvature, where a
race turns to allow
its beginning to
catch up with
its ending.
Finding
itself
run.

Blessed is the Fruit

For the memory of my mother

Hollow-eyed and midnight-pale, she hesitates
for reasons vastly unexplained.
The thin call quickening one of us
to her bedside.
'Who is that?' she asks,
moving her head in tiny validation of our birth.
Then falls away again, towards
the echoing abyss of delirium.
'She will not pass the night,'
the doctor says, hurrying
with his stethoscope at the door.
The priest arrives, and round her bed
in clumsy, half-circled vigil,
we seek comfort in the chant of meaningless refrain.
Afterwards, he tells her, 'Now you may sleep.'
To which she replies with sudden voice,
'And make sure I'm truly asleep
before they roast me.'
I glance at the priest, and on his lips
the fleeting smile
seduces a non-believer into prayer.

Goblins

Twenty metres away,
at eye level above the path,
something hovers on the air,
painted by the brush strokes of a setting sun,
and spinning inside the hollow flame of mystery.

It's a leaf. Trapped between the invisible membranes
of a spider's web, and twisting
with the flickering shape of something else.
Something on the edge of fear,
seen dimly, before the dawn,
like a child's bedtime story, unexplained.

But that first cold and rushing moment,
before knowing what it really way,
became part of a world long since abandoned.
A world of magic spells and witches,
and dragons off the edge of the map.
A world without reason, rationality or science.
Where things are clothed with the wonder
of heaven and hell.
And goblins all around.

Imagination

There is no shape, no closing wall,
no boundary fence to ride.
Its kingdom is that other world
where Gods are said to stride.

A fabled place of magic sails
that release our earthly tie,
and lift us high above the clouds
where we begin to fly.

Oh, flights of fearless fancy!
Such wondrous, soaring things.
How sweet it is to drift aloft
on a dreaming beat of wings!

To step inside a moment
that resonates with blue,
and there beside the endless sky,
come face to face with you.

The image of perfection;
the beauty of your birth.
To catch a glimpse of paradise,
before falling back to earth.

The Taste of Rainbows

For what becomes of innocence
worn down and lost in life?
The happy doubt of painful youth,
the calm and tempered strife.

The cosiness of winter dark,
the fey, unravelled thing;
the creative expectation
unanswered questions bring.

The universe is held aloft:
its mysteries lay unfurled,
but the night stars still outnumber
all the sand grains of the world.

And in the deepest mystery,
beyond microscopic reach,
rests the rainbow taste of wisdom
no scientist can teach.

And that's the way it should be;
untouchable and still,
with nothing but the shadow
of a light upon the hill.

Cassandra

She walks the valleys of my mind,
she sleeps inside my dreams.
She paints her pictures for the blind
with the silence of her screams.

She calls me from the river
where sweet waters always run.
She makes the daylight shiver
by turning back the sun.

She spins shadows of tomorrow
on looms of liquid lace.
She paints the shape of sorrow
upon her lovely face.

She sings her songs of glory
to those who cannot hear.
She writes the last great story
for those consumed by fear.

She bears the pain of ages
she does not question why.
She just turns and turns the pages
and wonders how to die.

Benediction

For Brian Cooper

We rest on sun-kissed stone a mountain high;
above Tilba Valley green and wide,
as a pair of eagles chase the sky,
like gods upon a rising tide.

We watch them fall through shining light,
wings outstretched and talons furled;
below us in their golden flight,
beyond the boundaries of our world.

They twist and fall and rise again,
a glorious swoop of rushing grace,
then dwindle on a distant plain,
inside the beauty of the place.

We retrace our steps down off the peak,
in single file with thoughts alone.
Knowing we will always seek
the memory of that sun-kissed stone.

The Playing Fields

A climate-change lament

This could have been a golden age
With reason claiming centre stage
To frame our fragile hopes with fluent grace
But hubris circled in
To roll dice with loaded spin
And desecrate the laws of time and space.

The playing fields of hopeful youth
Were swallowed by the doomsday truth
Of greed untethered from its pain
While corridors of power
Chanted progress with the hour
To crop a harvest coarsely cut across the grain.

Now deep inside the mystery
Of our reconstructed history
The hollow stuff of unremembered dreams
Haunts the road less travelled
To mourn a life unravelled
And chase its fatal loop of wasted schemes.

An Unsolved Crime

In fear and loss at leaving
the world in all its grieving,
he plummeted the winter cliff
released at last from mortal myth,
to drift upon a morning tide,
eyes and mouth all opened wide.
Horrified at having died.

The last great insult to his pride.

The Reverence of Apples

Shadows from a silence
On the cusp of what is known
Trace the twilight of forgiveness
Onto undiscovered stone.

And in the haven of this exile
Beneath a questing pulse of time
Whispered words of broken solace
Shape a half-remembered line.

Comfort me with apples
Sang the Bible long ago
Breathing hope from new beginnings
Going gently with the flow.

But now the Viper's tongue of reason
Has made the path too steep
And cast the Holy orchard
Into unrequited sleep.

Global Warming

In memory of climate change doubt and denial

Time passes as it always did,
flowers look the same;
birdsong greets the morning,
and someone shifts the blame.

Sunlight casts few shadows
in forests starved of trees;
and rivers choke with sediment,
as carbon rides the breeze.

Politicians vacillate;
science shakes its head,
religion seeks a higher plane,
and history makes its bed.

But none can bring redemption;
only echoes of the pain:
the bitter taste of our betrayal,
again…and yet again.

On Reading Poetry in Literary Magazines Today

The subtext screams 'no entry!'
– like razor wire on a high fence;
although here and there,
a phrase will cling
to the fingertips,
like breakfast marmalade
in some foreign hotel,
or a fabled landscape
glimpsed through a dusty window.
What's happening here?
I have a degree in Literature,
and read more books in one week
than most people read in a year;
I work with words,
but these precious poems,
with their closely feathered
inaccessibility, threaten to suffocate me.
Was this, I wonder – turning a page
in order to breathe – their intention?

The Sandbank

We are all of the same thing;
which at three in the morning
comes looking for answers.
And when you wake at this terrible
hour – the one Napoleon
so famously feared – you must go with the flow
as the expression fatuously declares,
smug within its own banality.
Like the drowning swimmer, surrendering
to a rip tide, until feeling the benediction
of a sandbank beneath both feet.

Because…
with our backs to the cosmic wall,
this is all we really are:
a chemical conundrum; wrapped in a myth;
sustained by our own fables, driven by ego –
and resting on a sandbank.
…waiting for infinity.

Gulaga Breathing

For Sean Burke, who, along with many others, defended the ancient forests near Gulaga, a mountain on the far south coast of NSW

A sacred light
On Gulaga bright
Draws breath within her dream
As the chainsaw roar of rushing night
Brings down a fatal scheme.

And a wasted sense
Of an immense
Commercially wanton need
Tramples any recompense
To satisfy our greed.

The angry sound
Of ravaged ground
Will rip the brooding air
And in green valleys all around
She'll weep in her despair.

As loose and fast
The die is cast
But if the trees should fall
Her truth will stand as something vast
And ours as very small.

To Write or Not to Write

When you need to write because you are –
and always have been – a writer,
but don't want to write because
you suspect there is too much
being written for the wrong reasons
by the wrong people, something dies.
Books and writing have become
marketing commodities,
driven by profit and ego; spawned
by a risible proliferation of writing classes,
and puffed into existence by spin.
To have once written but stopped
is tragedy personified: a yearning
for something that no longer seeks to be.

On being weary

I'm weary of having to tell people
I'm okay when clearly I am not;
weary of going along with the
unspoken assumption
that all this is merely an inconvenience,
like ingrowing toenails,
or a resistant dose of flue.
I'm weary of the sheer struggle
to get through day after day,
and (even worse) night after night
of being trapped inside a constant cycle
of anxiety and depression that is so unrelenting
it cannot be imagined – only lived.
I'm weary of the sense of irretrievable isolation,
where whatever I do or say,
has little chance of making anything happen
that might lessen the pain.
I'm weary of being part of a common perception
that this is something I should be able to shake off
by simply choosing to do so;
weary of the background implication
that it is all my own fault;
that it is somehow selfish and inconsiderate.
I'm weary of making jokes
at my own expense to mask the pain.
And I'm weary of being locked
inside an echo chamber
where everything is dulled
to the point of paralysis – except
the horror of knowing

my cerebral system is being quietly
hard-wired against the possibility
of escape.

Yes   I'm weary

So   unbelievably

weary.

Last lines

These tangled lines of where and when,
were written with a bitter pen.
Back and forth and round once more,
swept on by chance and hopeful sight;
washed up against a fragile shore:
a prisoner of the failing light.
Heaven-sent, the random wine,
Eros-carved, the silken dance;
like pleasures looted from a shrine,
they vanished with a backward glance.
I've paid my dues and set my sail,
there rests no debt against my name,
when morning breaks beyond the pale,
I'll stand before it with no shame.

Epitaph

A searching wind,
the constant sea,
this hungry world
has swallowed me.

The light is gone,
the day is done,
all passion spent,
and stories run.

The pages fall
without a mark,
and I am whispering
in the dark.

Acknowledgements

The preface to this collection is based on my essay published in *The Australian Literary Review* (volume 5, issue 1, February 2010) which, before being axed on economic grounds, appeared as a supplement each month in the national newspaper, *The Australian*. In previous weeks there had been a robust exchange of views on poetry in cyberspace as well as the letters column, and the then *ALR* editor had invited me to submit a 'provocative' opinion on the state of Australian poetry. My contribution was well-received – at least that was the impression given by many complimentary comments received in print and online – but an ominous silence from Ozpoetry insiders, the people I was mostly trying to reach, confirmed something I had long suspected: that they didn't really care about responses from outside the castle gates.

Shortly before writing the piece, I had crossed paths over cocktail drinks with an influential Ozlit identity, who wanted to know how I was going to approach the project. When it quickly became obvious that an intensely academic essay was expected, I shook my head and suggested that this had been done too many times already. Receiving a blank look in reply, I added that those essays were part of the problem rather than the solution, and reached for another drink as my questioner raised a critically cultured eyebrow and silently moved away.

I gratefully acknowledge that some of my poems were first published elsewhere: in print media such as *The Australian*, *The Canberra Times* or *Voice*, and various websites to do with contemporary issues such as refugee policy, the environment and other matters of social justice. Some were included in my collection of stories, essays and poems, *Evening at Murunna Point*, first published by Stephen Matthews of Ginninderra Press in 2001, and I would like to thank Stephen for giving this new collection a chance to see the light of day, as well as the team at Prinstant (Phil, Jeanne-Marie and Rick Tarrant) in Canberra for the production of the original edition in 2014.

Many of my poems reflect the crippling experience of clinical depression and anxiety disorder, and in closing I would like to express gratitude for support received over many years. Being linked by friendship or kinship to someone mysteriously wounded by such a persistently malignant – and largely invisible – illness is an intensely lonely and difficult journey that requires something as powerful as love to sustain it. Thank you.

www.ingramcontent.com/pod-product-compliance
Lightning Source LLC
Chambersburg PA
CBHW070907080526
44589CB00013B/1213